Mighty Bots

BATTLING ROBOTS

THOMAS KINGSLEY TROUPE

BLACK
RABBIT
BOOKS

BOLT

Bolt is published by Black Rabbit Books
P.O. Box 3263, Mankato, Minnesota, 56002.
www.blackrabbitbooks.com
Copyright © 2018 Black Rabbit Books

Jennifer Besel, editor; Grant Gould, interior
designer; Michael Sellner, cover designer;
Omay Ayres, photo researcher

Library of Congress Cataloging-in-Publication Data
Names: Troupe, Thomas Kingsley, author.
Title: Battling robots / by Thomas Kingsley Troupe.
Description: Mankato, Minnesota : Black Rabbit Books, [2018] | Series:
Bolt. Mighty bots | Audience: Ages 9-12. | Audience: Grades 4 to 6. |
Includes bibliographical references and index.
Identifiers: LCCN 2016049939 (print) | LCCN 2016051598 (ebook) | ISBN
9781680721577 (library binding) | ISBN 9781680722215 (e-book) | ISBN
9781680724608 (paperback)
Subjects: LCSH: Robots–Juvenile literature. | Robotics–Juvenile literature.|
Contests–Juvenile literature.
Classification: LCC TJ211.2 .T76 2018 (print) | LCC TJ211.2 (ebook) | DDC
629.8/92–dc23
LC record available at https://lccn.loc.gov/2016049939

Printed in the United States at CG Book Printers,
North Mankato, Minnesota, 56003. 3/17

Image Credits
Alamy: Historic Collection, 9
(top); INTERFOTO, 8 (top); Ken Howard,
8 (bottom); Pictorial Press Ltd., 9 (*Real Steel*);
REUTERS, 26; Xinhua, 14; AP Images: Eric Risberg,
22–23; Evgeny Biyatov, 6; Commons.wikimedia.org:
Kazuyoshi Kato, 27; Getty Images: Adam Taylor, 9, 12,
14–15 (spinners and thwacks), 18, 21; VASILY MAXIMOV,
15; VCG, 7; YOSHIKAZU TSUNO, 24–25; Robogames.net:
David Schumaker, 4–5, 17; Science Source: Philippe Psaila,
11 (bottom); Shutterstock: LOVIN, 26 (scale), 27 (scale);
MAX3D, 8–9 (background), 31; RFarrarons, 11 (top); The Life
Tre-e Project, 32; tsuneomp, 1, 3, 29, Back Cover; Volody-
myr Krasyuk, 10
Every effort has been made to contact copyright
holders for material reproduced in this book.
Any omissions will be rectified in subse-
quent printings if notice is given
to the publisher.

CONTENTS

CHAPTER 1

A Battling Robot......4

CHAPTER 2

Building Battling
Robots. 10

CHAPTER 3

Wired Warriors. 16

CHAPTER 4

Robots and
Humans. 25

Other Resources. 30

A Battling
ROBOT

Heavy machinery rumbles in the **arena**. The sound of crunching steel fills the room. A saw on one robot cuts at its **opponent**. The other robot flips through the air. It's a robot battle!

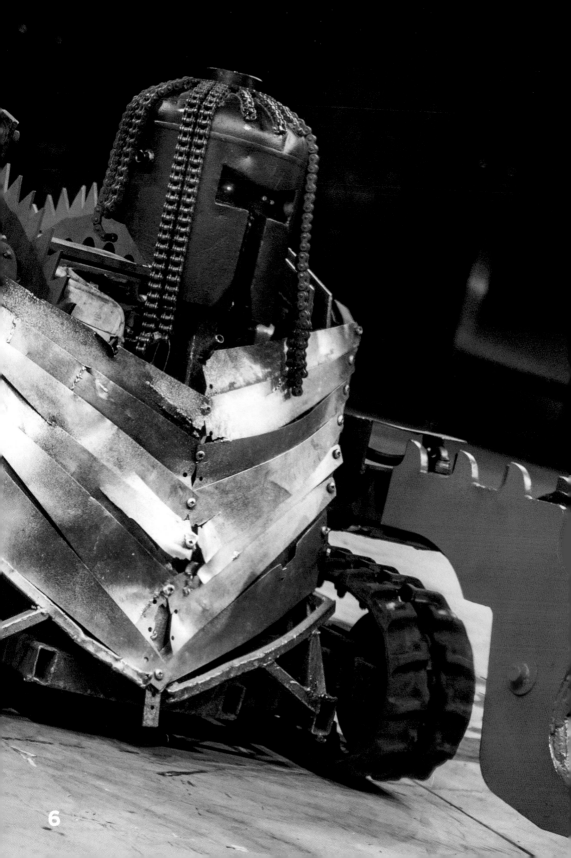

Rough Robots

Watching robots battle is exciting. People build battle bots to fight in competitions. They direct the robots' movements with remote controls. The robots' weapons cut, burn, and destroy.

ROBOT FIGHTING TIMELINE

Movies, games, and TV shows have captured the fun of battling robots.

1933
A cartoon shows Mickey Mouse training a robot to fight.

1974
In *Godzilla vs. Mechagodzilla*, Godzilla fights a robot monster.

1930

1964
The Rock 'Em Sock 'Em Robots game is released. Players make plastic robots punch each other.

1984
In *The Transformers*, alien robots come to Earth.

2000
In *BattleBots*, robot builders compete to destroy other bots.

2015

2011
In *Real Steel*, fans get involved in the new sport of robot boxing.

CHAPTER 2

Building Battling ROBOTS

Building robots isn't easy. But it's not just for scientists either. Building a robot takes patience, practice, and parts. But almost anyone can do it.

Basic Parts of Battling Robots

MOTOR AND BATTERY

TRANSMITTER AND RECEIVER

WHEELS AND FRAME

COMPLETE CONTROL

AIR
OPE

Weapons

Battling robots use weapons against each other. Builders add hammers and blades. Robots with **flamethrowers** really heat up the battle!

Not all weapons are allowed. Water and explosives are off-limits. **Devices that block remote control signals aren't allowed either.**

TYPES OF BATTLING ROBOTS

lifters and flippers
can lift and flip other bots

spinners
have spinning blades or spin their bodies

... thwacks

have hammers or axes

wedges
have sloped fronts

CHAPTER 3

WIRED Warriors

Robot battles are held around the world. Fans gather to watch the robots fight. Robots face each other in arenas. Their human controllers stand behind clear safety walls. In most competitions, battles are three minutes long.

Robot battles are dangerous. Judges watch battles from behind the safety walls too.

Total Destruction

During battles, bots crush, rip, and smash each other. Their controllers use the bots' weapons. The goal is to make the other bot stop moving. If a robot can't move for 10 seconds, it loses.

If one bot isn't stopped in three minutes, judges decide a winner.

Rules for Robots

Most competitions won't allow robots that blow things up. They also don't allow weapons that shoot bullets. These rules keep crowds safe. The robots aren't so lucky.

21

SIZING UP ROBOT WEIGHT CLASSES

POUNDS

225
200
175
150
125
100
75
50
25

FAIRYWEIGHT

0.3 POUND
(150 grams)

ANTWEIGHT

1 POUND
(0.5 kilogram)

KILOBOT

2.2 POUNDS
(1 kg)

BEETLEWEIGHT

3 POUNDS
(1.4 kg)

MANTISWEIGHT

6 POUNDS
(3 kg)

HOBBYWEIGHT
12
POUNDS
(5 kg)

BANTAMWEIGHT
15
POUNDS
(7 kg)

FEATHERWEIGHT
30
POUNDS
(14 kg)

LIGHTWEIGHT
60
POUNDS
(27 kg)

MIDDLEWEIGHT
120
POUNDS
(54 kg)

HEAVYWEIGHT
220
POUNDS
(100 kg)

CHAPTER 4

ROBOTS
and Humans

Battling robots are getting bigger and more amazing. Mk. II Megabot is a giant robot. Two humans ride inside. The robot's guns fire paintballs. The paintballs go more than 130 miles (209 kilometers) per hour.

Kuratas is another huge robot. It uses an **advanced** computer system. Its guns fire 6,000 BB pellets per minute.

15 feet
(5 meters) tall

Mk. II

WEIGHT

12,000 POUNDS
(5,443 kg)

26

about **13** **feet** (4 m) **tall**

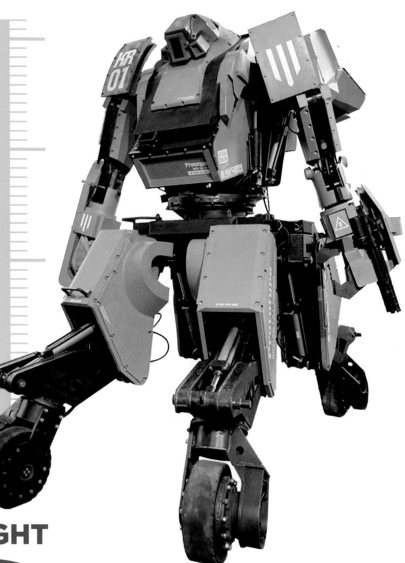

WEIGHT

9,000 POUNDS
(4,082 kg)

Kuratas

Future Fighters

Interest in fighting robots continues to grow. New technology helps make battling bots even better. Maybe someday, they will fight on their own.

GLOSSARY

advanced (ad-VANSD)—being beyond others in progress

arena (uh-REE-nuh)—an area for competition or other activities

device (dee-VIS)—an object, machine, or piece of equipment made for a special purpose

explosive (ik-SPLOH-siv)—able to cause an explosion

flamethrower (FLAYM-throw-uhr)—a weapon that shoots a stream of burning liquid

opponent (uh-POH-nunt)—a person, team, or group that is competing against another

receiver (reh-SEE-vur)—a piece of equipment used to convert signals into sound, light, or electrical signals

transmitter (tranz-MIH-tuhr)—a device that sends out radio or TV signals

BOOKS

Faust, Daniel R. *Building Robots: Robotic Engineers.* Engineers Rule! New York: PowerKids Press, 2016.

Larson, Kirsten W. *Hobby Robots.* Robotics in Our World. Mankato, MN: Amicus, 2018.

Swanson, Jennifer. *National Geographic Kids. Everything Robotics: All the Robotic Photos, Facts, and Fun!* Everything Series. Washington, D.C.: National Geographic, 2016.

WEBSITES

Robotics
kidsahead.com/subjects/1-robotics

Robotics: Facts
idahoptv.org/sciencetrek/topics/robots/facts.cfm

Robots for Kids
www.sciencekids.co.nz/robots.html

INDEX

C

competitions, 4, 7, 16, 19, 20

    judges, 16, 19

    rules, 13, 16, 19, 20

K

Kuratas, 25, 27

M

Mk. II Megabot, 25, 26

P

parts, 10–11

    weapons, 4, 7, 13, 14–15, 19, 20, 25

pop culture, 8–9

W

weights, 22–23, 26–27